"SEED FOR THE PLANTING"

By

E. Thomalen
www.ethomalen.com

"Seed for the Planting"

This play is a Drama based on the life of Kathe Kollwitz, a German artist, 1867 to 1945. The dialogue, mostly, has been fictionalized; although use has also been made of material from her diaries and letters. However, where such material has been incorporated, literary license has been exercised so that the material has been taken out of context and rearranged to satisfy the author's dramatic purposes. Although the play generally follows certain events in her life, these too have been altered, though as little as possible, to accommodate the drama. It is, thus, hopefully an evocation of her life and times rather than an absolutely faithful recreation of it. Much, of course, has been left out as well.

"Art is the funnel, as it were, through which spirit is poured into life."

Thomas Mann

Under Copyright 1984

USER AGREEMENT

You are only entitled to use the Content you obtained for your personal individual and non-commercial use. You are not permitted to make further copies or digital copies.

You agree that you will *not*: (a) use any Content (or any part thereof) for any commercial or non-personal purpose or otherwise use any Content other than in accordance with the above; (b) incorporate the Content (in whole or in part) in any other work or make an adaptations and translations of the Content (or any part thereof); (c) make any copies or reproduce such Content (or any part thereof) other than those expressly permitted; (d) issue copies of the Content (or any part thereof) or otherwise communicate the Content (or any part thereof) to the public; (e) perform, show, read aloud or play the Content (or any part thereof) in public; (f) rent, lend, distribute, publish, sub-license, assign, sell or otherwise transfer the Content (or any part thereof) to any third person; and (g) remove or modify any copyright or other proprietary notices contained in the Content.

The delivery of any Content to you does not grant you any commercial or promotional usage rights in the Content or any other rights (save as expressly stated in this agreement) all of which are hereby expressly reserved by us.

If you wish to copy or use any of this work for commercial or non-personal purpose further agreements with the author are required. Contact him through his website www.ethomalen.com.

PRODUCTION NOTES

"Seed for the Planting" was given its Premier Production at The Vagabond Players on July 9, 1987 directed by John Bruce Johnson with Christine Hohmann playing the role of Kathe Kollwitz. It was one of a group of plays chosen to be presented as part of the Baltimore Playwrights Festival VI. It was performed in a small 100 seat theater with a traditional proscenium arch. Use was made of the stage and the aisles to involve the audience in the play; slides of the artist's work were integrated into the production. Interest in the play developed after people became aware of the subject matter from the newspaper reviews and through word of mouth. Many people expressed disappointment that they were not able to see it a second time, due to the short run of the play (a total of 10 performances including opening night over three weekends). There was active interest among women's groups, peace groups, and the German community as well as members of the art community. Of some small interest is that four weeks after the end of the play, the major downtown public library had all of the Kollwitz biographical books out on loan.

"Kathe Kollwitz, a German expressionist artist who lived through and portrayed the horrors of two world wars, makes a fittingly dramatic subject in E. Thomalen's 'Seed for the Planting'...the play is the strongest entry thus far in the 1987 Baltimore Playwrights' Festival...'Seed for the Planting' introduces audiences to the individual behind some of the most powerful prints and sculptures to come out of Germany during the first half of this century. Mr. Thomalen shows us a woman who was brave in both her day-to-day life and in her work.

The play's title, 'Seed for the Planting must not be ground up' is a line from Goethe referring in this case to soldiers who died in combat, a subject that affected Mrs. Kollwitz artistically and personally (she lost a son in World War I and a Grandson in World War II)."

Baltimore Sun (1987)

"'Seed for the Planting' is must see summer fare...The set (incorporates) the artist Kollwitz's paintings as everchanging pictures on the walls. The audience is thereby given the opportunity to watch the progression of Kollwitz's work from its earliest light form of innocent youth through the years which brought her acclaim and recognition to the time when ...she showed the depression of the German people and led to her fall from favor."

Northwest Star (1987)

"SEED FOR THE PLANTING"

ACT I :   THE STAGE IS SET
Sc i: Kollwitz Apartment, Summer, 1943
Sc ii: Kollwitz Apartment, Summer, 1891
Sc iii: Kollwitz Apartment, Summer, 1892
Sc iv: A Large Party, Berlin,
Sc v: Hall outside Dr. K's offc., 1896
Sc vi: Berlin Street, 1899
Sc vii: Studio, Kathe Kollwitz, 1903

ACT II: THE GREAT WAR
Sc i: Berlin Street, 1914
Sc ii: Kollwitz Apartment, 1914
Sc iii: Berlin Street, late Oct. 1914
Sc iv: Kollwitz bedroom, 1917
Sc v: Union Meeting Hall, Summer, 1918

ACT III: THE DUEL

ACT IV: NAZIS COME TO POWER
Sc i: Hall outside Dr. Kollwitz office,
Sc ii: Kollwitz Apartment, July 1936
Sc iii: Kollwitz Apartment, 1938
Sc iv: Berlin Street, 1939
Sc v: Hall outside Dr. K's offc., 1940
Sc vi: Kollwitz Apartment, 1942
Sc vii: Kollwitz Apartment, 1943

Most of the action takes place in three scene settings, i.e., the Kollwitz apartment, a Hall outside Dr. Kollwitz office, and Kathe Kollwitz's studio. There are three large scenes, which need only be suggested in

their renderings, i.e., Berlin Street scenes,
Hauptman's large party and a Union Ha

Characters

(In order of appearance)

Driver - Ambulance
Kathe Kollwitz -Artist, Maiden Name
Schmidt
Jeep - Kathe's friend
Dr. Karl Kollwitz - Kathe's husband
Hauptman - German playwright
First Old Woman - Patient's of Dr. Kollwitz
Second Old Woman   - Same
Third Old Woman   - Same
Young Man   - Same
Young Woman   - Same
Middle Aged Man   - Same
Middle Aged Woman   - Same
Lina - Kollwitz's housekeeper
Midwife
Peter Kollwitz – Child, Karl & Kathe's
younger son
Citizens - Berlin Streets - 1914
Peter Kollwitz - Young Man
Walter Koch – Kollwitzs' friend
von Hindenburg - German general and later
President
Workers United Front
Nazi
Free Corps Volunteers- Demobilized former
soldiers
Young Man - Worker
Hans Kollwitz - Karl & Kathe's older son
Two Women - *Women's Int'l League for
Peace and Freedom*
Bankers
Young Woman- Int'l Workers Relief Org.
Social Democratic Party Member

French Ambassador
Soldier USSR
Director - Prussian Art Academy
Otto Braun - Prussian State Prime Minister
Newsboy
Director and Visitors to 1931 Art Exhibition
Radio Announcer
von Papen - Chancellor preceding Hitler
Herr Krug
Ottilie - Wife of Hans Kollwitz
Peter – Child, Son of Hans and Ottilie
Citizens in Berlin Street 1939

By having one actor play more than a single role it is possible, despite the large number of characters, to use under fifteen actors plus a child actor to play all of the parts.

ACT I

Scene i

(The place is the apartment of Kathe Kollwitz, 25 Weissenburgerstrasse at Worther Platz, Berlin, Germany, the time is the Summer of 1943. Kathe sits impassive, slumped against the back of her chair, staring into space. A man enters through an open door stage left wearing a Red Cross insignia on his German uniform, he is the driver to evacuate her from Berlin.)

DRIVER

Frau Kollwitz, you are the last to be evacuated -- I will help you down the stairs.

KATHE KOLLWITZ

Who are the others in the truck?

DRIVER

Three old women -- one in the front, two in the back.

KATHE KOLLWITZ

Where will you put me?

1

DRIVER

In the back.

KATHE KOLLWITZ

Do you think there will be a raid today?

DRIVER

They come every other day during daylight
hours now, there was none yesterday.

KATHE KOLLWITZ

Then I suppose we must hurry, where is my
cane to lean on, I would be lost without it.

DRIVER

You can put your weight on me.

KATHE KOLLWITZ

No, I must have it to carry my weight when
you are no longer around.

DRIVER

It's fallen behind the chair. I will get it for
you.

KATHE KOLLWITZ

Thank you.

DRIVER

Hurry now.

KATHE KOLLWITZ

I'm coming.

DRIVER

Take your time, I won't leave you.

KATHE KOLLWITZ

Thank you.

(After crossing the room to reach the door she hesitates.)

DRIVER

What makes you stop, is something forgotten?

KATHE KOLLWITZ

Forgotten? No... nothing.

(Still hesitating)

DRIVER

Have you left something behind then?

KATHE KOLLWITZ

Have I left something behind?

Scene ii

(The same apartment 50 (1891) years earlier, there is a knock at the door. Karl Kollwitz is reading and Kathe is putting flowers in a vase. Kathe goes to answer the door.)

KATHE KOLLWITZ

Jeep!

JEEP

Schmidt...

(Cocks head and laughs tentatively.)

Frau Dr. Kollwitz ... Kollwitz.. Frau Dr.

KATHE KOLLWITZ

What *is* it, Jeep?

JEEP

Excuse me, but you don't seem like a Frau Dr.

KATHE KOLLWITZ

You must still call me Schmidt as you did at the Art Academy.

DR. KOLLWITZ

But you are *married* now ... to me.

KATHE KOLLWITZ

You are so silly, Karl.

(She joins Jeep's laughter.)

DR. KOLLWITZ

What is so *funny*?

(They laugh harder.)

Are you laughing at me?

(They laugh still harder.)

Is my tie out of place? My collar? -- Does something that I'm wearing make me look ridiculous?

KATHE KOLLWITZ

Oh, Karl...

DR. KOLLWITZ

I *don't* understand your laughing.

KATHE KOLLWITZ

I know you don't.

DR. KOLLWITZ

I wish that you would stop -- my late afternoon patients will think us all mad.

(They laugh harder.)

Please will you come in!

(Jeep comes in and Dr. Kollwitz closes the door but they continue to laugh.)

Perhaps a glass of water will help you stop -- like with patients with hiccough --or if you hold your breath...

JEEP

The good doctor prescribes a cure for our mirth -- but the disease is too strong to respond to his remedies.

DR. KOLLWITZ

What is *wrong* with the two of you?

KATHE KOLLWITZ

He thinks something is wrong with us.

DR. KOLLWITZ

Please, please sit down and calm yourselves.

(Wringing his hands.)

The neighbors will report to the authorities that I cannot maintain order in my house.

(He closes a window.)

JEEP

Let them!

DR. KOLLWITZ

If you will not stop I will go out into the street to dissociate myself from it!

KATHE KOLLWITZ

Don't worry, nobody will connect *you* to it.

DR. KOLLWITZ

I am going all the same.

(Jeep and Kathe Kollwitz say Goodbye. He leaves.)

JEEP

(To Kathe.)

Pardon me Schmidt but your apartment seems so small.

KATHE KOLLWITZ

That's because it is.

(They fall into another round of hilarity.)

JEEP

In your letter you seemed depressed.

KATHE KOLLWITZ

Did you come to cheer me up?

JEEP

Don't forget what's mine is yours and what's your is mine.

KATHE KOLLWITZ

You can *have* him.

JEEP

He seems like a dear man!

KATHE KOLLWITZ

He *is* a dear man.

JEEP

Are you pregnant?

KATHE KOLLWITZ

No, thank God!

JEEP

Have you given art up yet?

KATHE KOLLWITZ

Never!

(Door opens.)

DR. KOLLWITZ

I'm *back*.

KATHE KOLLWITZ

Karl's back.

(The laughter increases again.)

DR. KOLLWITZ

I have made a diagnosis.

JEEP

He knows what's wrong with us.

DR. KOLLWITZ

(Smiling.)

You are both suffering from fatigue and that has lowered your strength and most importantly the mental ability to control yourselves.

(Laughter increases.)

In your case, Jeep, it is from the long trip and Kathe, you have been working too long hours on your etching!

KATHE KOLLWITZ

(To Jeep.)

He wants me always home to fix his dinner!

DR. KOLLWITZ

I know the trouble even if you won't admit it!

KATHE KOLLWITZ

Shall we agree with him?

JEEP

Why not?

DR. KOLLWITZ

I know the only remedy for it. I am going to put you both to bed. You don't even need to take off your clothes.

KATHE KOLLWITZ

Are you putting us to bed like Mama?

JEEP

At least when he puts us to bed as naughty children, he doesn't spank us.

DR. KOLLWITZ

There -- now rest and we will talk sensibly in the morning.

Scene iii

(The same apartment two years later. Karl Kollwitz is reading and Kathe is writing a letter. At the end she holds up the image of Plate: 2.)

KATHE KOLLWITZ

Dear Jeep: How I miss you at this time. What a pretty baby Hans is. I feel so fulfilled. I still manage to do some etchings, which are coming along but caring for the baby is restricting, although a joy. New life fills me with the greatest hope for immortality, my other talent I am less certain of. The baby has brought Karl and me closer and he is helpful, and considerate

10

of me. He was anxious for me while I carried it, but also worried whether we could afford a child on what he earns. Sometimes I have felt quite alone, but not now. I have Karl, and Hans too! I feel I have more in common with my own Mother, and can understand some of her feelings, and her great strength. Like when my baby brother Benjamin was dying with meningitis, and the old nurse threw open the door calling out to my Mother as she did: "He's throwing up again, he's throwing up again." My Mother, who was ladling the soup out to the rest of us, stiffened, for a moment, and then continued her task. She knew, of course, what it meant, for she had lost our oldest brother Julius of the same thing. Yet she did not allow it to distract her from taking care of the rest of us, although her feelings, after carrying the child for nine months in her body, which no man can know, must have been of the most intense kind of grief. I admire her for her stoicism, and am in awe of it. Sometimes, when I saw my own first born in the crib, that awful thought passes through me: What would I do in similar circumstances. But I quickly turn it out. I do not know if I would have my mother's strength. Then I think of Karl, oh poor, dear Karl, he would do his duty regardless, of that I'm sure. How I envy that in him, he holds it in like she did also. Well, I don't wish to burden you with more of these gloomy musings of mine. I look forward to seeing you soon, you always have the most positive effect on me!

> With Love,
>
> Schmidt

Scene iv

(A large party in Berlin, a few years later).

KATHE KOLLWITZ

Excuse me, Herr *Hauptman!*

HAUPTMAN

Yes, certainly, my dear young woman.

KATHE KOLLWITZ

Do you remember me?

HAUPTMAN

You look familiar yet ...

KATHE KOLLWITZ

Julie....Hofferichter.

HAUPTMAN

Yes, yes, now I know. You are her *younger* sister. It has been a while!

KATHE KOLLWITZ

Ten years. We still talk of that party. It was my first trip to Berlin, so exciting to find my older sister knew, even then, Germany's *foremost* modern writer, and to be *invited* to his house...

HAUPTMAN

You are very kind. Was that not the party I gave for the painters Schmidt and Holz? Yes it was! And you were there, so young and pretty -- quiet, yet sensitive, with the intention to be an artist too, I believe.

KATHE KOLLWITZ

That you remember me at all, I take as the highest flattery!

HAUPTMAN

Are you still working at it?

KATHE KOLLWITZ

I am but the work is hard.

HAUPTMAN

For us all.

KATHE KOLLWITZ

I want to tell you that I so much enjoyed your play.

HAUPTMAN

Thank you . . . But Paris was better, one didn't have to hide from the police there.

KATHE KOLLWITZ

When Jaeger says: "Why tell me, Emily, are you in service in high society now? Well, then, see to it that you get out of here. The wind might start blowing around here one of these days and it'll blow everything away -- overnight". I thought that you were talking to me! Jaeger speaks to all of us who are young, we must *listen*. The older ones won't listen, and the wealthy ones, who exploit the workers, have learned nothing in 50 years.

14

HAUPTMAN

You give them credit. They have learned nothing in 500 years!

KATHE KOLLWITZ

You are right! My brother is a Socialist. When I came to Berlin the first thing that he showed me was the graves of those who had died in the 1848 uprising in Berlin. It was a moment I shall *never* forget. We stood together in silence to honor them.

HAUPTMAN

A toast to the March dead!

(All in the circle raise their glasses.)

KATHE KOLLWITZ

And to the Weavers also!

(The toast is repeated.)

HAUPTMAN

My grandfather was a weaver in Silesia.

KATHE KOLLWITZ

Was he?

HAUPTMAN

Yes, yes and my Father was an innkeeper and often told stories about him. They were a miserable lot and got by I do not know how. In the end they were shot down but at least they had their say for awhile.

KATHE KOLLWITZ

I feel sympathy with them too.

HAUPTMAN

You said your brother is a Socialist, is this he?

KATHE KOLLWITZ

No, no. This is my husband, Dr. Karl Kollwitz -- he is a Health Insurance Doctor.

HAUPTMAN

I am so pleased to meet you Herr Doctor.

DR. KOLLWITZ

The pleasure is mine *entirely*.

HAUPTMAN

Did you see the play?

DR. KOLLWITZ

I would have liked to, but my schedule of patients would not permit it.

HAUPTMAN

Well, at least you came tonight and I am grateful for that.

DR. KOLLWITZ

It has been my pleasure *again*. I have read
your work and admired it.

HAUPTMAN

Thank you. Please excuse me I must see to
it that the new arrivals are welcomed.

DR. KOLLWITZ

Do you think he was offended that I missed
the performance of his play?

KATHE KOLLWITZ

Of course not, Karl, he understands a
doctor's schedule.

DR. KOLLWITZ

Good, I am relieved.

KATHE KOLLWITZ

This is an evening I shall never forget, it is
as though I can see and almost touch
Germany's future and it is *here* in this room.

Scene v

(Three old women enter a hall that is used as an overflow waiting area for Dr. Kollwitz's patients. There are two doors visible, one leads to Dr. Kollwitz's office, and the other to Frau Kollwitz's studio. They are separated by two rough wooden benches that are nearer Dr. Kollwitz's office, and can seat three persons each. Four places are taken, two by a middle age couple, and one each by a young man and a young woman. The young man is seated alone on the bench furthest from Dr. Kollwitz's office, and he gets up so that the three old women can occupy that bench. Only the First Old Woman has eyeglasses to see where she is going. They are bent over, dressed in black and wearing shawls.)

FIRST OLD WOMAN

You might have been quicker about it! *(They all nod.)*

YOUNG MAN

Be thankful with my back I did not stretch out full length upon that bench waiting for the Doctor!

SECOND OLD WOMAN

(Peering at him through the glasses she borrows from the first.)
You probably injured it falling off a bar-room stool.
(They cackle at this fine joke.)

YOUNG MAN

I'm sorry now I gave up my place to the likes of you! I don't have to stand here and put up with such insulting remarks.

THIRD OLD WOMAN

What will you do about it, then?

YOUNG MAN

I ... I don't know, I might leave.

FIRST OLD WOMAN

He has forgotten about his back so soon, the doctor's work is done for him already. Could it be you came here just to get a day off of work?

YOUNG MAN

What do you, old women, know about work anyway?

SECOND OLD WOMAN

What do *you* know about it?

(They cackle.)

YOUNG MAN

More than *you* I'm sure.

THIRD OLD WOMAN

Your wife will never see the money you make at it.

YOUNG MAN

What would you know about my affairs anyway?

SECOND OLD WOMAN

We know.

YOUNG MAN

Has my wife been complaining about me again? I'll have a word or two with her about that when I get home!

FIRST OLD WOMAN

When you leave here with the doctor's slip you won't get by the first tavern you see, and by the time you get home you will be too *drunk* to remember anything.

YOUNG MAN

We'll see about that!

YOUNG WOMAN

Why do you provoke this man, who has been kind to you?

SECOND OLD WOMAN

What business is that of yours anyway?

YOUNG WOMAN

He is a fellow suffering human being.

THIRD OLD WOMAN

Is that all?

YOUNG WOMAN

What do you mean?

FIRST OLD WOMAN

Or are you looking for a customer, if so you'll find he is a good one!

YOUNG WOMAN

(To the man.)

Just ignore these hags; their dispositions are uglier, even, than their faces.

YOUNG MAN

I will pay them no mind, thanks for your kind word.

SECOND OLD WOMAN

You had better watch out, she has the disease.

YOUNG MAN

They cannot stop meddling in the affairs of others and are no doubt universally detested for it. Maybe you will be kind enough to catch a disease yourselves, serious enough to die from, and we shall be rid of you. It cannot come soon enough for me.

THIRD OLD WOMAN

When we strip away the pretty wrapping, we find the sour lemon underneath.

YOUNG MAN

(To young woman.)

Come, let's you and I take a walk, and return later after *they* are gone.

YOUNG WOMAN

Indeed, why should we be forced to endure their bad manners?

(They leave.)

FIRST OLD WOMAN

Sisters, we got rid of them.

(Cackles),

Now we must sit still until the Doctor comes.

SECOND OLD WOMAN

The Doctor's our good friend.

THIRD OLD WOMAN

And he doesn't even know it.

FIRST OLD WOMAN

Shh, Sisters, -- Shh -- He'll come soon.

THIRD OLD WOMAN

What gives you the right to tell us what to do?

FIRST OLD WOMAN

Am I not the oldest?

THIRD OLD WOMAN

What of it?

SECOND OLD WOMAN

Sisters, why do you always fight?

THIRD OLD WOMAN

Stay out of this, it is between us.

FIRST OLD WOMAN

She can speak. I'm sure she agrees with me.

It's you who always must be different!

SECOND OLD WOMAN

I don't agree with *either* of you.

THIRD OLD WOMAN

You must *choose* one of us.

SECOND OLD WOMAN

Why must I? You both are stupid!

THIRD OLD WOMAN

(To second old woman.)

She puts on airs.

(To first old woman.)

You always have something mean to say.

FIRST OLD WOMAN

(To second old woman.)

Don't you think it is *her* that is not civil?

(The door of Kathe Kollwitz's studio opens and she comes out obviously pregnant and near term. She walks down the hall away from the three women and off stage.)

SECOND OLD WOMAN

Isn't that Frau Doctor?

(Each takes a turn looking through the one set of eyeglasses.)

FIRST OLD WOMAN

How can anyone bring a child into the world in these times?

SECOND OLD WOMAN

These times are not so bad.

FIRST OLD WOMAN

They will get worse, much worse, she is a fool.

SECOND OLD WOMAN

You always have a *pessimistic* view.

FIRST OLD WOMAN

You know it as well as I.

THIRD OLD WOMAN

No man or woman knows what will be before it happens.

FIRST OLD WOMAN

The signs are clear enough!

MIDDLE AGED WOMAN

Why do the three of you say such *unpleasant* things?

MIDDLE AGED MAN

Yes, you even criticize the wife of our dear Doctor.

MIDDLE AGED WOMAN

The doctor's fault is he is too kind-hearted to turn away such miserable ones as you. You cannot get along with each other or anyone else. Come Wilhelm we will come back later too.

(They leave. Off Stage.)

KATHE KOLLWITZ

(Groans.)

Is she here yet, the midwife?

LINA

Yes, she's come!

MIDWIFE

How are you, Frau Doctor?

KATHE KOLLWITZ

I think the baby's coming!

MIDWIFE

Quite right -- everything is proceeding nicely. I see the head -- there it's out and now the shoulders and the rest of it.

(The baby cries.)

26

Ah, it's a boy, and a beautiful one at that. There now, I will clean him up and give him to you to hold. Someone get the Father *quickly* now that the women's work is done. What will you call him?

KATHE KOLLWITZ

Peter!

MIDWIFE

My, my, a grand name for such a little boy. Two sons, yes, yes how *fortunate* you are.

FIRST OLD WOMAN

Now she has *two* sons.

SECOND OLD WOMAN

Two indeed, she bore two sons to give her double joy!

THIRD OLD WOMAN

But one will give her joy and one sorrow blacker than the blackest night.

SECOND OLD WOMAN

How shall she tell which is which?

THIRD OLD WOMAN

At the birthing they're all alike and all that matters then is whether they spring forward quickly or linger on the way.

FIRST OLD WOMAN

Of the rest, merciful God knows but keeps it
to Himself.

Scene vi

(l899 A street in Berlin, Plates: 3,4,5,6)

JEEP

Schmidt, Schmidt, I heard the news!

KATHE KOLLWITZ

Yes, yes, it's true!

JEEP

You won the gold for the Weavers series in
Dresden.

KATHE KOLLWITZ

Yes, yes, my "Children of Sorrow" won the
prize.

JEEP

Such *sorrow*, I wish I had it!

KATHE KOLLWITZ

It has made me known overnight.

JEEP

You well deserve it! You would have won it last year at The Berlin Exhibition if Adolf Menzel had had his way.

KATHE KOLLWITZ

The Kaiser was more interested in what his advisors of State had to say than his advisors on art!

JEEP

(Laughing.)

Maybe he'll have cause for his concern. Besides he is no better at judging politics than he is at judging art!

KATHE KOLLWITZ

The King of Saxony doesn't worry so much about politics.

JEEP

He has less to worry about.

(They both laugh.)

KATHE KOLLWITZ

The Berlin Exhibition was good for me anyway; it gave me a chance to earn a little money.

JEEP

Five Hundred Marks -- you call that little?

KATHE KOLLWITZ

No, no, I did not mean it that way. In fact, I could not believe that someone would offer that much for just one print and not the plates as well.

JEEP

It's a lot of money to you and me, but not to those rich folk who can afford to buy it.

KATHE KOLLWITZ

They are not usually interested in social protest art, just Kitsch.

JEEP

If they buy it, it's because they recognize it's worth, and hope to sell it later at a handsome *profit*!

KATHE KOLLWITZ

Do you think all collectors are like that?

JEEP

It's the way the world is.

KATHE KOLLWITZ

You may be right, that's sad.

JEEP

Cheer up, it's brought you something nice-- ignore the rest. You and I alone can't change the world -- but maybe something will, *eventually*.

KATHE KOLLWITZ

I share your hope for that.

Scene vii

(1903. Kathe, in her apartment, is sketching Jeep who is posing for her. Peter, now seven years old, is, himself, drawing a military toy horse and rider which he has placed on a table in one corner. Plate: 7)

JEEP

I'm tired. This is an awkward pose.

KATHE KOLLWITZ

Just a little longer.

JEEP

No! I've had enough!

KATHE KOLLWITZ

It is still not right.

JEEP

Then you must be content with it for now.
(She puts down her arms.)

KATHE KOLLWITZ

Very well.

JEEP

What are these poses for?

KATHE KOLLWITZ

I am trying to draw a woman with a dead child in her arms.

JEEP

What? Don't use *me* for it. I don't want to be the model for such a thing. It might bring bad luck. What makes you do a sketch like that anyway?

KATHE KOLLWITZ

Children of working class mothers die all the time -Karl sees them in his practice, and tries his best, but even he cannot always prevent it.

JEEP

They have large families.

KATHE KOLLWITZ

It doesn't matter. It hurts just as much, large or small.

JEEP

Well, leave it to Karl, why are *you* so preoccupied with it just now?

KATHE KOLLWITZ

It nearly touched me close to home.

JEEP

What do you mean?

KATHE KOLLWITZ

Peter is always sickly with his TB, but it was Hans that *nearly* died. He had Diphtheria with a high temperature and bad sore throat. Karl saw the greyish patches on it and tried a new serum that he heard of. At first it worked like a miracle. The fever went down and Hans could swallow better. The brightness returned to his eyes and his whole body regained its joyfulness. Then he relapsed, suddenly, and went down further then he had been at any time with this illness. His fever was high; he could not swallow even a little soup. He implored us to help him with his eyes, and whimpered a little when the pain was terrible, but he was too weak to cry. Karl and I stayed with him, taking turns, and, finally, at 3 A.M., when Karl came to bed, he said he thought he'd won him back. I could not sleep, but kept waiting for the door to open, and Karl to say ... "he's gone". I don't know what I'd have done; I have never known so awful a fear. I felt so helpless too, there was nothing I could do for him. When Karl came to bed I sat up in Hans' room the rest of the night and listened to his breathing, prayed that the illness would not return, and, if a life was needed, to take mine. He recovered completely after that night but *I* have not been the same. I cannot get the picture out of my mind ... of a dead child ... and it follows me everywhere, even into sleep. I guess it is the reason I must complete this drawing -- to get it out of me -- if only onto paper.

JEEP

I must go, I cannot help you with it. Goodbye.

KATHE KOLLWITZ

Wait ... I understand.

(Kisses her on the cheek)

Goodbye and thank you for modeling for me, it is such a help.

(After Jeep leaves Kathe sits in front of a mirror in a pose like Jeeps'. Then she sketches and poses again, repeating this a number of times. Peter comes over.)

PETER

Do you like my picture, Mother?

KATHE KOLLWITZ

Peter it is very nice, but you haven't got this leg of the horse here quite right -- it should be a little shorter than the other.

PETER

Thank you. I will try to do it better, Mother.

KATHE KOLLWITZ

Wait a minute, Peter.

PETER

What is it, Mother?

KATHE KOLLWITZ

Come here I want to hold you.

PETER

Like this?

(Standing he puts his arms around his Mother's neck.)

KATHE KOLLWITZ

No, Peter -- I want you to lie in my arms.

PETER

Like so?

(He climbs into her arms and lies out straight rigidly)

KATHE KOLLWITZ

No, Peter -- loosened --like you were... *asleep.*

PETER

Oh.

(He becomes limp in her arms.)

KATHE KOLLWITZ

Yes, that's right.

(She looks at herself in the mirror.)

That's enough, now get down.

PETER

Can I go back to my drawing?

KATHE KOLLWITZ

Yes, for a minute but I may need you again.

(*They both sketch.*)

Once more, Peter.

(*He comes over again.*)

PETER

Like this?

KATHE KOLLWITZ

Yes, that's it.

(*She groans form the weight.*)

Ohh.

PETER

Don't worry, Mother, it will be beautiful, too.

ACT II

Scene i

(June 28, 1914, A Street in Berlin.)

FIRST MAN

Have you heard the *news*?

SECOND MAN

What news?

FIRST MAN

The Archduke has been shot!

SECOND MAN

The *Archduke* -- where?

FIRST MAN

In Sarajevo!

SECOND MAN

Is he dead?

FIRST MAN

They think so.

SECOND MAN

Those Serbs, they should be punished -- they're responsible for it!

FIRST MAN

They will be, the Emperor will see to that.

SECOND MAN

The Kaiser must support a fellow German, even if he is an Austrian.

FIRST MAN

He will, have no fear! There's been no real *military* action since '71.

(The stage clears. Then popular dance hall music is heard and the stage gradually fills with excited happy people.)

FIRST WOMAN

Isn't it *wonderful?*

SECOND WOMAN

It *is* wonderful!

FIRST MAN

People dancing, yes indeed! Let Germany's enemies see with what enthusiasm her young men are eager to fight them. Let them think that over, and consider the benefit a peaceful Germany is to them.

SECOND MAN

Aye, they should think about *that*, they should -- especially the meddling Czar, and the French. They will regret they did not answer the Kaiser more *politely*, more to his liking. They'll have the German people to answer to for it now!

FIRST MAN

The Army recruiters can't get down all the names fast enough!

SECOND MAN

The dance halls, and the taverns, are doing a holiday business, and the pretty girls are giving each boy going off a flower!

FIRST MAN

This is a time to be alive, to see all Germans stand together, rich and poor, young and old, right and left, alike.

SECOND MAN

Our boys will be drinking champagne in Paris before the leaves are down -- I've no doubt of that. Ha. Ha.

FIRST MAN

And Nicholas will ask for German forgiveness -- he will get it for a price -- Russian caviar to go with the French champagne.

SECOND MAN

What about the English?

FIRST MAN

What about them? Ha. Ha.

FIRST OLD WOMAN

Excuse me. Excuse me.

SECOND MAN

Old ladies, old ladies, kick up your heels,
dance together if you cannot find men your
age!

SECOND OLD WOMAN

We see no cause to dance.

FIRST MAN

Germany's declared war on Russia, and
France - is that not reason enough?

THIRD OLD WOMAN

We'll see, we'll see.

SECOND MAN

Let's go down to the station and see off the
newest volunteers. I wish I was their age,
to go with them myself.

*(A three-piece German oompah band playing
German marches appears. Gradually the
young and the old fall in behind it, and
march off stage leaving behind only the
three old women.)*

FIRST OLD WOMAN

They dance now to the beat of the music and the drum.

SECOND OLD WOMAN

But soon they'll hear only the beat of the cannon and the gun.

THIRD OLD WOMAN

Aye, and these streets will echo faintly with the muffled sounds of parent's grief in place of the public utterances of joy!

Scene ii

(Shortly afterward, the Living Room of the Kollwitz's apartment. Karl, Kathe and Peter are engaged in an argument. All are standing, Peter nearest the door. Kathe leans against a table.)

PETER

But I want to go!

DR. KOLLWITZ

You are only eighteen, Peter.

PETER

I can go if you will *sign* for me.

KATHE KOLLWITZ

Wait six months; if you still want to go, we will sign the papers then.

PETER

Why six months?

KATHE KOLLWITZ

I don't expect the war to last that long.

PETER

I *knew* it!

KATHE KOLLWITZ

Healthy men, whole men, will be needed to work in Germany.

PETER

I want to fight for my country, like my friends are doing!

DR. KOLLWITZ

You might be killed.

PETER

If so, it is an honorable death, to fight and die for Germany, for the German people!

KATHE KOLLWITZ

Ask your Father if dying is so wonderful, he has seen plenty of it! There is precious little worth giving up one's life for.

PETER

I don't care, I want to go.

DR. KOLLWITZ

Be reasonable.

PETER

No!

DR. KOLLWITZ

Why are you so bent on it?

PETER

All of Germany is rallying to the defense of the Fatherland. Look at the people in the streets!

KATHE KOLLWITZ

They are fools -- I weep for them.

PETER

Even the socialists in the Reichstag voted for the war! High and low it's supported.

KATHE KOLLWITZ

It wouldn't have mattered to the government if they had disagreed.

PETER

Yes, but they *didn't*! Everybody must do his duty in a time of national danger. Father sees more patients now, to take up the slack left by younger doctors who have volunteered. Even you go out and work in public kitchens to feed the poor, relieve others to fight when war comes -- everybody must take his place, mine is at the front!

DR. KOLLWITZ

Why, why must it be there?

PETER

That's where everyone my age is!

DR. KOLLWITZ

Youthful passion overcomes good sense.

PETER

The only reason that you don't want me to go is that you are too old to go yourself, and maybe I shall do something you have never done!

KATHE KOLLWITZ

That is *not* a kind thing to say to your Father.

PETER

Well, he deserves it.

KATHE KOLLWITZ

And why don't I want you to go then?

PETER

You won't admit I'm grown up.

KATHE KOLLWITZ

I have no doubt of it -- I've had no doubt for a long time.

PETER

I'm sorry then, but if I'm grown up I should be able to make my own decision!

DR. KOLLWITZ

Oh, Peter, *Peter* -- matters like these are not so easy to decide, people in the clinic *often* turn to me with it.

PETER

I don't care about *them*; I shall start here deciding for myself!

KATHE KOLLWITZ

This seems more stubbornness, than reasonable judgment.

PETER

You didn't object to Hans going!

DR. KOLLWITZ

We couldn't, he is of age.

PETER

It bothers you to have to give your permission for me, doesn't it -- to share the risk with me so to speak? Well, I swear by God in Heaven that it is *my* decision, and you are free of all blame and responsibility for the outcome of it. There, does that satisfy you? You are blameless! On my head alone fall the consequences. Now, *please*, sign the papers for me.

KATHE KOLLWITZ

Your absolution will be little comfort if you are killed or wounded.

PETER

What if something happens to Hans?

KATHE KOLLWITZ

It would be awful!

PETER

But maybe he will become a hero instead.

DR. KOLLWITZ

The Generals get the medals, Peter.

PETER

Why must you always be a cynic?

DR. KOLLWITZ

I cannot say anything to make you happy!

PETER

Hans did it -- he has volunteered -- I want to go *too*.

KATHE KOLLWITZ

"Hans did it." "Hans did it." It always comes down to the same thing. "Hans did it". I'm tired of that!

PETER

Then let me go!

KATHE KOLLWITZ

Hans enlisted but he is three and one-half years older than you, and, if I may say so, more reasonable, and better able to take care of himself.

PETER

So *now* it comes out -- you still think I am a child -- well I will show you -- I can take care of myself -- you don't have to worry -- maybe even better than Hans!

DR. KOLLWITZ

Peter -- be reasonable!

PETER

I am, *you* are not.

KATHE KOLLWITZ

Sometimes it takes being more grownup not to do what everybody else is so anxious to do.

PETER

I can see through that argument, it is just another tactic to try to get me to give up what I want to do! Would you accuse Hauptman of just going along? He has tweaked the Kaiser's nose more than once. But he supports the war! He supports the Army!

KATHE KOLLWITZ

We need you here!

PETER

Oh, yes, fine. But I need to be at the front!

KATHE KOLLWITZ

You are an artist; Peter, you have great skill. I know. I have watched it grow as you have grown. You have something to give to the world. Don't waste it, Peter, I beg you, don't waste it. I plead with you, not only as a mother with her son, but as a respectful fellow artist. Your country *needs* you, Peter, but *not* as a soldier.

PETER

Yes, yes, Mother. I want to be an artist but how can I be a fine artist if I stay at home and experience *nothing*? What will I have to say, who will even listen to me, how will I know what is the truth? No. Mother, I respect you, and if you truly respect me as an artist, as a colleague, then you will let me go. Otherwise, I shall be just an insignificant scribbler, useful only to decorate parlors and drawing rooms, but with nothing profound to say to the world, or to anyone. You made your choice, Mother, let me make mine!

KATHE KOLLWITZ

Peter, you wear us down, you exhaust us.

PETER

Then give in, and rest.

KATHE KOLLWITZ

You seem so certain of your choice.

PETER

I am and I will not give up until you sign the papers!

KATHE KOLLWITZ

(Turns away from Peter and Karl.)

Shall we continue to hold out, Karl? I don't know. Maybe he is right, maybe I am wrong. Everybody agrees with him. Sometimes, when I transfer a sketch I have made to the lithographer's stone, fate takes a hand; and alters it, for better or for worse. So maybe it is here. My own instincts are against it, but his character, and God's doing, bring about changes beyond my power to control.

Scene iii

(Late October, 1914 the Kollwitzes are walking one way and another man, Walter

Koch, is walking the opposite way on a Berlin Street. Plate: 8.)

DR. KOLLWITZ

Walter Koch, how are you?

WALTER KOCH

Good day, Karl, Kathe.

(Tips his hat...they pass each other and Walter Koch turns around)

Karl...

(The Kollwitzes both turn around)

I have come from the Red Cross building, I don't know if you know... Peter's name...is on the lists...

KATHE KOLLWITZ

Is he wounded?

WALTER KOCH

Oh, God...I'm the one to tell you...He's been...killed. He died in Belgium,..in the first wave.

DR. KOLLWITZ

Are you *sure*? Are you certain?

WALTER KOCH

Kathe, you look faint, are you all right?

KATHE KOLLWITZ

Yes. I'm all right, I think. I'm all right - I think!

Scene iv

(A night, 1917, Kathe and Karl Kollwitz are in bed. One of the three old women sits on the chest of each of them while the third stands at the foot of the bed. All of the old women then withdraw to the walls of the room and Kathe gets out of bed and skips gaily around the end of the bed. Plate: 9.)

KATHE KOLLWITZ

One boy to the right, and one to the left, my right son, and my left son . . we dance when Spring arrives.

(Looking to the right)

Peter what I'd like to see in you is the beginning of thorough study. As you yourself said, as soon as you start on color, that's the end of studying. I am happy about your way of seeing forms; I think you see what is organic. But your color is an emotional outpouring. And one can allow oneself emotional outpourings only after strenuous intellectual effort. If the emotional outpourings come first, you soon get a fluttering feeling in your stomach; you have a hangover. And then a feeling of dilettantism. We shall be quarreling over this point, time and time again. But for the present, we agree that training is necessary. If one only knew what training first; and where. I have not seen your self-portrait in its earliest stages. As it is now, it strikes me as tortured. It would have been better had I not always, conscientiously, looked the other way when I came into your room. Peter! Where is he?

(She stops.)

FIRST OLD WOMAN

Dead.

KATHE KOLLWITZ

Dead? I was just talking to him!

SECOND OLD WOMAN

Dead, in the war.

KATHE KOLLWITZ

War? What war? I haven't heard of a war.
There are threats yes, but there is no war!
It is the state of affairs in Europe today.

THIRD OLD WOMAN

In Belgium!

KATHE KOLLWITZ

That is absurd. Peter was not planning a
visit to Belgium. He would have told me he
was going!

THIRD OLD WOMAN

Dead!

KATHE KOLLWITZ

Where did this baby come from? Is he
mine? I wasn't aware of another pregnancy
... all the old tenderness. . an inexpressibly
sweet, lovely, physical feeling, a very small
baby, exuding all the warm bodily
fragrances of babies, a feeling of great bliss.
Oh, oh, nothing to fret about.

(Humming Brahms lullaby, she rocks him.)
There, there. Do you belong to me? I keep
dreaming of babies. Are you Hans or . . .

FIRST OLD WOMAN

Peter!

KATHE KOLLWITZ

Don't say it!

SECOND OLD WOMAN

Or Peter...

KATHE KOLLWITZ

This child isn't dead. Maybe I have had a child after Peter. I still have two sons, one to the left and one to. . .

THIRD OLD WOMAN

Peter!

KATHE KOLLWITZ

Mother...who died? Was it Grandfather Rupp? He was so deep, so profound. Who will take over his Church? He taught us in religious class:

(Imitating a loving stern grandfather)

Man is not meant for happiness but to do what is required of him. Do you see Mother how he has even engraved it on his tombstone? He continues to teach us still! But was he *right*, Mother? How much *is* required of us, Mother, how *much*, and can

56

we have no say in it? But he was a good man; he lived a long life and had a devoted congregation. But was he *right*, Mother? What is this, a letter?

FIRST OLD WOMAN

'Your Son...

KATHE KOLLWITZ

My Son?

SECOND OLD WOMAN

"Has been killed in action..."

KATHE KOLLWITZ

I am only seventeen. I don't have any children!

THIRD OLD WOMAN

'On the field of honor...'

KATHE KOLLWITZ

Peter, you industrious little farmer! Is the elderberry already blooming? It's wonderful that you are working so hard in the fields, my boy! Too bad I cannot eat some of your rhubarb, and your peas. Not even some of the strawberries, when they ripen...

(Pause)

Formerly, I did not look to either side. Now I find myself vulnerable, sometimes I am prey to despair. And I am too much upset by the young people, with their different points of view. Now, I already belong to the *older* generation, to those who have been long arrivee', and are blocking the way and taking the light from the youth. It is interesting, this eternally rising wave of the youngest youths. They cannot be understood by the more mature artists, by those who have technique, and craftsmanship, for they almost never possess any special superiority. All their superiority lies in the young people's imagination. Show seasons are, naturally, always disturbing because I see all the strange, youthful and new things passing before me, and they excite me. I compare them with myself, and see, with disgusting clarity, what is feeble, and reactionary, in my own work! Here the difference in generations becomes apparent. I have to *work* to sympathize with them. Their experiences are not interesting to us. Perhaps they would be if these young people opened themselves, but they do not do that! Suppose for me, too, all that was left of life was to look on? I want to live, and work, while the daylight lasts. I do not want to shut my eyes, but to create a counterpoise to the horror, the pain.

FIRST OLD WOMAN

Where is Peter?

KATHE KOLLWITZ

In the garden.

SECOND OLD WOMAN

Did you taste what he offered?

KATHE KOLLWITZ

I could not, I was away.

THIRD OLD WOMAN

You shall never taste it again!

KATHE KOLLWITZ

No! Please . . What is this? It is a ram for sacrifice, and next to it a sharp knife. Yes, I understand. All God required of me is that I be *willing* to sacrifice my son, if He demanded it. That is all! It is all He required of Abraham! *See*, at the last minute He has granted me my son as He granted Isaac to Abraham. He shows that He will accept another offering in place of a *human* sacrifice, in place of a *son*. Praise God! Take this, for I make it willingly. There, it is done!

FIRST OLD WOMAN

It is *Peter* across whose throat you drew the knife!

KATHE KOLLWITZ

You are mistaken!

SECOND OLD WOMAN

Look for *yourself*

KATHE KOLLWITZ

It is a beast that eats grass in the field.

THIRD OLD WOMAN

Your *son* is dead.

KATHE KOLLWITZ

Can I *endure* it? "Jesus last words were 'My God why hast Thou Forsaken me?' When just before he has said his proud: 'Or thinkest thou that my Father cannot send me more than twelve legions of angels'.

And in Gethsemane: 'If this cup may not pass away from me except I drink it, Thy will be done'. That is, at the beginning he showed complete acceptance of destiny, because it must be so. Perhaps something similar to what I experienced in my petty human relationship, when I gave Peter and he died. Then I, too, could not manage to say everything had to be so, but rather: 'My God, why hast thou forsaken me?'. In my secret heart I had probably expected that I would not be forsaken. And perhaps Jesus was not prepared for his Father's refusing to send the legion of angels; and I, too, secretly expected there would be provided a ram for the sacrifice. Why was Abraham just taken at this word? Why was it enough for him just to *show* he was willing? Jesus was willing enough. But when He hung on the cross: 'Why hast thou forsaken me?'" But I will not forsake God, and I will not forsake Peter! Peter will not die needlessly; his cause will be my cause. He believed in Germany and went into her Army of his own free will. I could not stop him. He is dead. I must not be a bitter old woman and criticize or complain, it would not be what he wished. I will not break faith with him; I will pick up the torch he dropped.

FIRST OLD WOMAN

There are now five million dead.

KATHE KOLLWITZ

I cannot *bear* it.

SECOND OLD WOMAN

More than five million ruined.

KATHE KOLLWITZ

Is it a breach of faith with you, Peter, if I can now see only *madness* in the war?

THIRD OLD WOMAN

Peter's friends: ... Eric, ... Walter, Meier..., Gottfried, ... Richard ... now ... *all* dead.

KATHE KOLLWITZ

No! They were the "Seed for the Planting"!

DR. KOLLWITZ

(Gets up and gently puts his arms around Kathe.)

Aren't you going to come to bed...and sleep...?

Scene v

(1918. The Scene takes place in a Union Meeting Hall in Berlin in the late summer of 1918. There are mostly middle-aged men and women and an occasional younger person with crutches or a cane. An intense, earnest man is addressing the crowd. Kathe Kollwitz and Dr. Kollwitz sit in the middles and the three old women are seated in the back. Only their speech may be heard.)

FIRST OLD WOMAN

The war on the Eastern front is won.

SECOND OLD WOMAN

The Armies that were there have been sent into France.

THIRD OLD WOMAN

And they advanced again as in 1914 to the Marne.

SECOND OLD WOMAN

Now, as then, they have been pushed back. There are no more armies for Germany to call upon for help.

FIRST OLD WOMAN

Her enemies multiply, daily the list of them grows longer, while her friends turn to her for help and are no help themselves.

SECOND OLD WOMAN

Wait, this man calls for more young volunteers to go to the front again and save Germany once more!

THIRD OLD WOMAN

All fit young men, the flower of her youth.

FIRST OLD WOMAN

To sacrifice themselves for Germany; if necessary.

SECOND OLD WOMAN

The leaders of the young, teachers and poets, all call for it, and stand firmly, even fervently, behind it!

THIRD OLD WOMAN

A woman stands up.

FIRST OLD WOMAN

Is it not Frau Kollwitz?

SECOND OLD WOMAN

What does she say?

FIRST OLD WOMAN

She speaks of a poet greater than those living. *Goethe*, I think.

KATHE KOLLWITZ

There has been enough of dying! Let not another man fall! Against the poet that you invoke I ask that the words of an even *greater* poet be remembered, "Seed for the planting must *not* be ground up"!

THIRD OLD WOMAN

Good words.

SECOND OLD WOMAN

Wise words.

FIRST OLD WOMAN

Well intended.

SECOND OLD WOMAN

Well meant most certainly!

THIRD OLD WOMAN

But who can see the next planting?

SECOND OLD WOMAN

And who the *harvest* that follows it?

FIRST OLD WOMAN

Man saves the seed in hopes.

SECOND OLD WOMAN

And hope makes disappointment still more bitter!

THIRD OLD WOMAN

Who can see the calamities that may come?

SECOND OLD WOMAN

Germany's river of sorrows will become a sea.

FIRST OLD WOMAN

Partly of her own making; partly not.

SECOND OLD WOMAN

Who could believe it?

THIRD OLD WOMAN

Who would believe the present is *not* the worst?

SECOND OLD WOMAN

Even the wise words of men can be confounded!

THIRD OLD WOMAN

And well-considered actions undone.

FIRST OLD WOMAN

Unseen things hide in the present.

THIRD OLD WOMAN

Terrible things, unimagined by good people!

FIRST OLD WOMAN

Even their worst dreams would stop short of it!

SECOND OLD WOMAN

Do not underestimate the worst of mankind.

FIRST OLD WOMAN

Weep for the good.

THIRD OLD WOMAN

Better still; warn them!

SECOND OLD WOMAN

They cannot hear.

FIRST OLD WOMAN

They *will* not hear.

THIRD OLD WOMAN

Or see.

ACT III

Scene i

(The Duel: 1918 – 1933. Far downstage center is a small round table with a red and black checkerboard and checkers placed for the start of a match. The scene opens with General von Hindenburg alone on stage.)

VON HINDENBURG

(Re-reading a telegram he is preparing to send)

To the government in Berlin: Repeat, *War cannot be won*. Request an immediate armistice or it will mean downfall of the nation. The army will have to surrender. Signed, General von Hindenburg, Chief of the General Staff, German Armed Forces. *(He leaves and Kathe Kollwitz enters.)*

DR. KOLLWITZ

Have you heard?

KATHE KOLLWITZ

What?

DR. KOLLWITZ

An armistice has been signed.

KATHE KOLLWITZ

At last!

DR. KOLLWITZ

I was beginning to think that it would *never*
come.

KATHE KOLLWITZ

November 11, 1918, Peace and Freedom!

DR. KOLLWITZ

The world will remember this date; the end
of "war".

KATHE KOLLWITZ

Let us hope so. But it must be nourished.
*(She goes over to a checkerboard. A band of
workers appear singing the United Front
Song adapted from Bertolt Brecht.)*

WORKERS

Because a man is a man

He'll want to eat, thanks a lot;

But talk can't take the place of meat

Or fill an empty pot.

So, left! Two! Three!

So, left! Two! Three!

Comrade there is a place for you

Stand with the worker's Front

For you are a worker too.

And because a man is a man

He'll not be cowed by a blow to the face

He wants no bondservant beneath him

Nor above him a blood sucking class.

    So, left! Two! Three!

    So, left! Two! Three!

    Comrade there is a place for you

    Stand with the workers' Front

And because a man is a worker,

No one else can bring him liberty.

It's no one else but the workers own

Work that will set him free!

    So, left! Two! Three!

    So, left! Two! Three!

    Comrade, there's a place for you

    Stand with the workers' Front

    For you are a worker too!

(A Nazi enters stage left, the Nazi and Kollwitz begin a game of checkers. Kathe Kollwitz plays the red pieces and the Nazi plays the black ones. Several young army veterans enter stage left. They are Free corps

FREE CORPS VOLUNTEERS - ALL

The Free Corps Brigade smashes everything to bits;

Watch out you Proletarian sons-of-a-bitch!

FIRST VOLUNTEER

Our patience is short; our anger is deep;

You wanted some rest; this rifle will help you to sleep.

SECOND VOLUNTEER

Don't try to think for yourself; do what you're *told*!

Or your eyes will become dim and your body grow cold.

THIRD VOLUNTEER

Steel in the *gut*, a small shot of *lead*,

And you will give up all those dreams in your head!

FREE CORPS VOLUNTEERS - ALL

The Free Corps Brigade smashes everything to bits;

Watch out you workers sons-of-a-bitch!

(They march off stage, there are shots. The Nazi moves his checker. A young man enters stage right. Plate 10.)

YOUNG MAN

Frau Kollwitz?

KATHE KOLLWITZ

Yes?

YOUNG MAN

I want you to know that, although I am a Communist, I do not agree with the party; that because you are not a party member you should not have been permitted to do the Memorial Litho. of Liebnecht our martyred leader.   Death to the "Free Corps"; but to you love, and respect! May we sell prints at the 1920 Workers Art Exhibition to provide funds for artists and workers in need?

KATHE KOLLWITZ

Of course! I shared his vision for Germany, of peace and social justice. I would be glad to contribute what you can use.

YOUNG MAN

Thank you!

72

(He leaves, Kathe Kollwitz counters the Nazi's move on the checkerboard. A Free Corps volunteer reenters and speaks to the Nazi at the table.)

NAZI

We have added our 555th party member in 1920 with our slogan 'Germany Awake!'. He is a corporal in the barracks in Munich.

(He leaves, and the Nazi makes another move at the table. The phone rings and Kollwitz answers it.)

HANS KOLLWITZ

Hello, Mother?

KATHE KOLLWITZ

Hans, is it you?

HANS KOLLWITZ

Yes, Mother. Mark July 9, 1921 down in your diary! Ottilie and I have had a *son*. It is a boy, Mother.

KATHE KOLLWITZ

Oh, Hans how wonderful -- your first born -- but what is his name?

HANS KOLLWITZ

We have both agreed -- it's *Peter*; Peter, Mother. You have lost one but we have brought another to life to wipe away your tears.

KATHE KOLLWITZ

(Tears fall down her cheeks.)
Oh, Oh, Hans...

HANS KOLLWITZ

I have to get back to Ottilie, Mother. I hope you will be able to come soon to visit.

KATHE KOLLWITZ

Yes, Hans, we will! I will tell your Father and he will be pleased too.

(She hangs up, returns to the board and makes a confident reply to the Nazi's move...Hindenburg reappears on stage.)

VON HINDENBURG

I will *not* answer any questions before this committee in regard to why Germany lost the war. I only repeat what an English general said to me: that the German Army did not lose the war on the battlefield, but was *stabbed in the back* at home. No, I do not deny that I asked for the armistice, and believed that Germany could not win the war. But the government in Berlin signed the Armistice, and the Peace Treaty. The Army is not responsible for them. What is that? Did they have any alternative? Don't ask me, I am only a general who did the best he could to defend his country. I won't answer any more questions. No, I won't tell you who the English general was. *What*? It's up to you whether you believe it or not! No! I have nothing further to say. Thank you. Gentlemen. Good day!

(The Nazi makes a move on the checkerboard.)

FIRST WOMAN

Will you join?

SECOND WOMAN

I don't know...

FIRST WOMAN

Kollwitz is a member. Have you seen her antiwar woodcuts?

SECOND WOMAN

Yes. Very strong! *The Woman's International League for Peace and Freedom*, but what can *women* do?

FIRST WOMAN

Did you *see* Kollwitz work?

SECOND WOMAN

Yes...I, I will join!

(Kollwitz moves her checker to counter the Nazi's piece...Two bankers enter stage right with top hats, monocles and cut away coats.)

FIRST BANKER

Our enemies seem to think that we will *meekly* accept war guilt, loss of territory *and* reparation payments. It is *too much*!

SECOND BANKER

You are right! Yes. You are right; it *is too much*!

FIRST BANKER

If we allow the currency to inflate ...

SECOND BANKER

But they are demanding 132 *Billion* Marks.

FIRST BANKER

If we allow the currency to inflate excessively, exorbitantly, then 132 Billion Marks may only buy them a few loaves of bread. Let them be satisfied with that!

SECOND BANKER

But what will it do to our own people?

FIRST BANKER

What does it matter as long as it strikes back at *them!* Besides, it won't hurt the propertied class, only the wage slaves, the small money lending Jews, and the pensioners who drain the public treasury.

SECOND BANKER

We bankers have our ways, we can be more subtle than the generals, but no less effective.

(They shake hands, and the Nazi makes another move. A young woman enters, shabbily dressed, with a handful of red carnations for Frau Kollwitz. Plate 11)

YOUNG WOMAN

Frau Kollwitz

KATHE KOLLWITZ

Yes.

YOUNG WOMAN

I have brought you these.

KATHE KOLLWITZ

Thank you, but why have you brought them?

YOUNG WOMAN

I come on behalf of the *International Workers Relief Organization* and myself. You, at least, have seen our misery and told it to the world in the poster: "Hunger". If they do not help, woe to us all!

KATHE KOLLWITZ

They will, they must, this is 1923! Thank you, my child.

(The girl leaves and Kollwitz answers the Nazi's move. The three old women enter.)

FIRST OLD WOMAN

I think its because the French and Belgians violated German sovereignty, and occupied the Ruhr.

SECOND OLD WOMAN

No, I think it is because of the inflation, two billion marks to buy a loaf of bread. It is *impossible.*

THIRD OLD WOMAN

I think it may be that he was copying that Italian.

SECOND OLD WOMAN

The police in Munich let him get away with *unfurling* his party's banners, in defiance of the authorities! What can one expect?

FIRST OLD WOMAN

Now he tries a Putsch!

SECOND OLD WOMAN

And he calls the government ministers in Berlin the "November criminals" for signing the armistice. But isn't *he* the criminal for committing crimes against the state?

THIRD OLD WOMAN

How can an ordinary citizen know what is right? What to believe?

SECOND OLD WOMAN

I say that how the *judges* decide it will tell. If he gets a hard sentence then they believe the government is right, but if he gets a light one, then you can draw your own conclusion.

(They exit and the Nazi makes another move. A young Social Democratic Party member comes over to Kollwitz. Plate: 12)

SOCIAL DEMOCRAT

Frau Kollwitz?

KATHE KOLLWITZ

Yes?

SOCIAL DEMOCRAT

I have been sent by the Social Democratic Party in Leipzig. We need a poster, for our rally asking 'Never Again War', at the German youth day in Leipzig. It will mark the tenth anniversary of the start of the last, *awful* war. We need something that will counter the lift the Right has gotten from the publicity, and short sentences, that the Nazis have received! We are afraid the youth will be won over by the militarists!

KATHE KOLLWITZ

I will see what I can do.

SOCIAL DEMOCRAT

Thank you, Frau Kollwitz. We need it for the rally on August l, l924.

KATHE KOLLWITZ

It will be ready!

(The Social Democrat leaves and Kollwitz makes a move on the board. The French Ambassador enters)

FRENCH AMBASSADOR

Urgent cable to government in Paris: It appears that the Germans have elected wartime General von Hindenburg President in the runoff election of l925. Stop. Will the Germans never learn? Stop.

(The Nazi jumps one of Kollwitz checkers. A messenger dressed as a soldier from the U.S.S.R. arrives.)

SOLDIER U.S.S.R.

Are you Kathe Kollwitz?

KATHE KOLLWITZ

Yes.

SOLDIER U.S.S.R.

Pleased to meet you.

(Shakes her hand vigorously, then steps back to attention.)

I have come on behalf of the government of the U.S.S.R. to invite you to attend the Tenth Anniversary Celebration of the Communist Revolution in Russia. There is to be a three-day exhibit of art in Moscow as part of the celebration; and your work, with your permission of course, has been chosen to be included. You are invited to attend as an official guest of the State.

KATHE KOLLWITZ

It will be my honor to accept. Although I am not a Communist, I have been excited by what the Communist Party has been trying to do in Russia.

SOLDIER U.S.S.R.

The exhibition will be in November, 1927!

KATHE KOLLWITZ

Yes, I know, thank you. I look forward to it.

SOLDIER U.S.S.R.

Goodbye.

KATHE KOLLWITZ

Goodbye.

(She returns and jumps the Nazi checker on the board. A clean-shaven man with glasses, dressed in a suit enters.)

DIRECTOR

As the new Director of The Prussian Academy of Art in Berlin it is my *privilege* and *pleasure* Frau Kollwitz to appoint you, in the year of 1928, to the head of the Graphics Department! I hope that you will accept.

KATHE KOLLWITZ

It is a great honor!

DIRECTOR

Good. You are to teach the masters graphics class as part of your duties. There will, of course, be a studio and a small stipend to go with the post.

KATHE KOLLWITZ

I look forward to it!

DIRECTOR

Very well, then, it's done!

(He turns, and leaves. Kathe Kollwitz makes a second jump on the checkerboard. Then

OTTO BRAUN

Frau Dr. Kollwitz, I am pleased to present to you the highest Prussian award to a civilian, once only given to soldiers for conspicuous bravery on the field of battle. This high honor, *'Pour la Merite'*, was inaugurated by Frederick the Great; as every Prussian schoolboy knows. In 1929, you are the recipient. Congratulations!

KATHE KOLLWITZ

Thank you very much. I am indeed deeply grateful.

OTTO BRAUN

Your stature in Germany is assured! You have achieved what few men, and fewer women, have ever attained. By virtue of your achievement, recognized by this honor, you shall be revered by all Germans for the rest of your life; and your work shall gain wider and wider recognition and acceptance! You, by your art, lead us into a new era of peace and betterment of all people.

KATHE KOLLWITZ

I humbly thank you.

(He leaves and she returns to the board, making one more jump. Then a newsboy enters.)

NEWS BOY

Extra! Extra! American stock market crashes. Experts fear damage to the world economic system. Extra! Extra! American stock market crashes. Extra! Extra!

(He leaves, the Nazi begins a series of jumps. Another Nazi comes on stage from stage left and speaks to Kollwitz.)

NAZI

We are now the second largest party in the Reichstag. In 1930 we won more than six million votes versus one million in 1928. We won't forget those who don't go along!

(The Nazi makes another jump. A number of people enter stage right.)

DIRECTOR OF EXHIBITION

This is the night of the unveiling of Frau Kollwitz "Memorial to the Fallen".

(Nods toward it)

The work is powerful.

MIDDLE AGED WOMAN

Yes, but depressing. We have left all that behind, why must we be reminded of it again in 1931? The war is part of Germany's past. I say let it rest in peace. Joy is best to seal the painful catacombs of the heart! Works of cheerfulness are desired, not this.

MIDDLE AGED MAN

I don't know; I like it.

YOUNG MAN

My brother died and my parents still have not gotten over it.

YOUNG WOMAN

You never get over something like that; thank heavens my son survived!

OLD MAN

Where are the sculptures of the broad shouldered German soldier who gave his life, bravely, on the field of honor while the Socialists...

OLD WOMAN

You are a militaristic old *fool*. This work is the finest work by an artist of the war -- it is a fitting monument. When you send young men to war, you create an even vaster army of such people as these, in cities and towns across Germany. If you once thought of that, you might not be so hasty to cry for "war" and "volunteers". In the end, an army of such people will rise up and strike you down, and all your cannons, and guns will not stop them. They have nothing more to lose. Frau Kollwitz, as an artist you deserve congratulations, as a person, my deepest sympathy.

(People file out, offering congratulations. Kollwitz makes a jump on the checkerboard. A radio announcer appears.)

RADIO ANNOUNCER

Meinen Damen und Herren, Good evening. My voice is coming to you over radio Berlin in the German capital. Tonight, we will bring you Otto Klemperer conducting, and the Berlin State Opera performing, Alban Berg's: *Wozzek*. But first the news! These are the results of the voting for the second Presidential Election. As expected, Reich's President von Hindenburg won, getting 53% of the votes. However, Herr Hitler made a surprisingly strong showing, gathering 36% of the vote. The Communist party candidate only received 10%. The Reich's President's victory was attributed to the fact that the parties of the center, and the left, except the Communists, supported him against the Nazi candidate. And now we will go to the State Opera House for tonight's important performance!

(Kollwitz makes another jump on the checkerboard. Then the newsboy reappears.)

NEWSBOY

Extra! Extra! Read all about it. Hindenburg dismisses the Chancellor of the center party, says that he has to move to the right. He asks von Papen to form a government. Von Papen dissolves the Reichstag, and lifts the ban on the Nazi brown shirts. Extra! Extra!

(The Nazi now makes a jump. Two women appear.)

CITIZEN

Did you see the poster urging the Communist Party and the Social Democratic Party to form a united front against the Nazis?

CITIZEN

Yes. Kollwitz name was on it along with Einstein and Mann.

CITIZEN

Will they heed it?

(Kollwitz makes a jump. The radio announcer reappears.)

RADIO ANNOUNCER

Tonight, I bring you the results of the voting for the *sixth* Reichstag on July 31, 1932. The Nazi party has made astonishing gains in this election. Herr Hitler's party has grown from winning only 2% of the deputies in 1926, 19% in 1930 to winning 38% in 1932, and becoming the *largest* party in the Reichstag. Most observers attribute this to an inability of the parties of the left to work together in the campaign. This evening we again go to the State Opera for a performance of *Salome* by Strauss!

(The Nazi makes another jump. President von Hindenburg and former Chancellor von Papen enter stage left.)

VON HINDENBURG

Franz von Papen, how *are* you? How is my good cavalry officer?

VON PAPEN

Well, thank you, and the Reich's President?

VON HINDENBURG

Well, too, thank you. This country air agrees with me; better than what is in Berlin.

VON PAPEN

It is cleaner, truer here. People are not so ready to cut each other's throats, eh?

VON HINDENBURG

Indeed, Franzchen, indeed! I am indebted to my friends for such a fine gift. It certainly gives me a different perspective on German politics from here.

VON PAPEN

It is nothing. You have given dedicated service, as General of the Army and President, shouldn't some of your *friends*, at least, recognize that, and at *no cost* to the Federal Treasury? The Kaiser would have rewarded you with this estate had he not been forced to abdicate by the *Bolsheviks*.
(The Nazi makes another jump.)

VON HINDENBURG

The Kaiser was a fine man, a fine man.
(Wipes his eyes.)
Well, what brings you here?

VON PAPEN

I hear that General Schleicher has been unable to form a government.

VON HINDENBURG

That is correct!

VON PAPEN

I have a Chancellor for you.

VON HINDENBURG

Franzchen, Franzchen, I would appoint you in a moment but 62 deputies out of 584 ...

VON PAPEN

No, that's not it.

VON HINDENBURG

What then?

VON PAPEN

I have met with the Nazi party leader at the home of the banker Kurt von Schroder in Cologne. The industrialists are ready to support him.

VON HINDENBURG

That Bavarian *corporal*?

VON PAPEN

He controls 196 deputies in the Reichstag and the alternative would be an opening to the *left* again.

VON HINDENBURG

I know Franzchen, but...

VON PAPEN

I think it can be done.

VON HINDENBURG

How? How can it be done? This is what I want to know! *How* can it be done? What does he *want*?

VON PAPEN

He wants to be Chancellor.

VON HINDENBURG

Aach! A street agitator? Representing Germany with the French and the English? A Nazi in the Ministry of Foreign Affairs ...

VON PAPEN

He doesn't demand that. We can put somebody reliable in that post.

VON HINDENBURG

Ja?

VON PAPEN

He has agreed to accept them.

VON HINDENBURG

The Wehrmacht will never accept a Storm Trooper telling its generals what to do.

VON PAPEN

He is willing to concede that ministry too.

VON HINDENBURG

What *does* he *want*? Finance? What do the Nazis know about it, one minute they join with the Communists in a city strike, the next they make alliances with the Industrialists. Or Transport? Or Commerce and Agriculture? Welfare? What?

VON PAPEN

He is willing to concede all of the *important*, the *desirable* ministries. He is even agreeable to myself as Vice Chancellor.

VON HINDENBURG

Maybe you can keep him reigned in. But he cannot want the Chancellorship of Germany so badly that he is willing to give away *all* of the ministries in his cabinet! What does he want?

VON PAPEN

Only the ministries of the *Interior*, and the *Prussian State*. What will he have? Education! The Courts! The Police! The Hospitals! He will have to stop all the street brawling. These are *not* ministries where anything *important* can be done that will raise his standing at the polls.

VON HINDENBURG

I *see* what you have in mind!

VON PAPEN

I think that he can be *safely* contained. They will have to police themselves.

(The Nazi makes another move. Then the three old women enter reading a newspaper. After each speaks a page of the newspaper is turned.)

FIRST OLD WOMAN

Frau Kollwitz signs an appeal for joint action by all parties of the Left to prevent Hitler from coming to power.

(Kollwitz makes a jump.)

They do not heed it.

SECOND OLD WOMAN

January 30, 1933 Hitler becomes Chancellor.

(The Nazi makes a jump.)

THIRD OLD WOMAN

The Nazis call for new elections in March. In the voting six days after the Reichstag fire the Nazis increase their delegate strength.   They have a *majority* after arresting the Communist deputies.

(The Nazi makes two jumps.)

SECOND OLD WOMAN

The Third Reich opens in March when Hitler passes the "Law for Removing the Distress from the People and the Reich" which gives him dictatorial power and suspends the Constitution.

(The Nazi overturns the board.)

ACT IV

Scene i

(1933. The waiting room outside of Dr. Kollwitz's office.   The three sisters are waiting with one other well-dressed man. Dr. Kollwitz appears.)

DR. KOLLWITZ

Herr Krug.

(He motions to him to enter the consulting room.)

FIRST OLD WOMAN

A better class of people come to see our doctor now!

(Gives a disapproving look, then gets up and goes over to the wall to look at one of Kathe Kollwitz's lithographs)

SECOND OLD WOMAN

But not so many of them.

THIRD OLD WOMAN

The Nazis have taken away his appointment.

SECOND OLD WOMAN

He sees whom he can.

FIRST OLD WOMAN

And who will pay.

SECOND OLD WOMAN

He must get by!

THIRD OLD WOMAN

He is not used to it.

SECOND OLD WOMAN

Not many wealthy ones live in a workingman's district.

FIRST OLD WOMAN

Nor would they come to see him here.

SECOND OLD WOMAN

He sees the poor too, but must turn some of them away.

THIRD OLD WOMAN

He will not turn us away.

SECOND OLD WOMAN

He has known us too long for that.

FIRST OLD WOMAN

They will remove Frau Kollwitz's work from among the living.

SECOND OLD WOMAN

And will try to cut her off from the dead as well!

THIRD OLD WOMAN

Some have tried to help.

SECOND OLD WOMAN

Her friend Jeep's husband was willing to write to Goering on her behalf.

FIRST OLD WOMAN

She wouldn't have it!

SECOND OLD WOMAN

Many will suffer for their principles.

THIRD OLD WOMAN

They have searched her home.

SECOND OLD WOMAN

And that of her son! And taken away his position too, and he has a wife and four children to feed.

FIRST OLD WOMAN

Hauptman has gone along!

THIRD OLD WOMAN

To many he is a traitor for it!

SECOND OLD WOMAN

No one calls him that out *loud*; others too have gone along.

FIRST OLD WOMAN

Or fled the country.

SECOND OLD WOMAN

Their dear ones left behind must pay for it!

THIRD OLD WOMAN

Aye, with their lives and their children's lives.

SECOND OLD WOMAN

Now in Germany it is best to be a childless orphan with nothing one calls dear.

Scene ii

(July, 1936. Kathe Kollwitz is putting some flowers in a vase in the Kollwitz apartment. There is a knock at the door and she opens it. At the door is a Nazi SS Officer. He is then, of average height but his officer's cap is high and broad giving his face a death's head appearance. He gives the Nazi stiff-armed salute.)

NAZI

Heil Hitler!

KATHE KOLLWITZ

Guten Morgen.

NAZI

Frau Kollwitz, we talk at last!

KATHE KOLLWITZ

What is it that you want?

NAZI

You did not listen to me in 1930.

KATHE KOLLWITZ

I could not *help* hearing you.

100

NAZI

You did not pay *attention* though, I warned you, and you did not take heed of it. My informants, and they are everywhere, have told me that you attend funerals of Jews.

KATHE KOLLWITZ

Max Lieberman was my friend. Is it a crime in Germany now to attend funerals?

NAZI

You should be more careful whom you pick as friends.

KATHE KOLLWITZ

He was a distinguished painter and once directed The Academy.

NAZI

But he was a Jew!

KATHE KOLLWITZ

You have seen to it that I have lost my post at The Academy, taken away my studio and my stipend, have decreed my work cannot be sold in Germany and removed it from display in museums and exhibitions. Now you tell me that I cannot go to the funerals of my friends!

NAZI

You have been punished for your views, but, *also,* for your friends! Jews and Bolsheviks are enemies of the State, and we shall be rid of them. You seem to be fond of associating with our enemies. Shall we ignore that, shall we let that pass, and be accused of the weakness of our predecessors? Do not believe it for a moment! We will act! You will see! Have you seen the latest issue of *Izvestia*?
(Hands her the paper).

Your name is mentioned in it. The reporter, a Bolshevik, I need not remind you, writes of an interview with you, that is not entirely flattering to Germany, and this government. Now, shall I let it pass, shall I let foreigners have a view of us that is biased, while the good, the truth about our regime, goes unreported? We cannot have that! And, another artist is mentioned, who was also present at that meeting, but his mane is *omitted.* No doubt a careless oversight; doubtless, not conspiratorial. But we would like to know who he is, so that we might help him gain a more "balanced" perspective of German life under The Fuhrer. Unfortunately, we cannot question the reporter who is back in Moscow, so we must learn *his name* from you. Therefore, I have come today, not about the small matter of the passing of a Jew, but the larger matter of slanders in the foreign press!

KATHE KOLLWITZ

I have only spoken what I see as the truth.

NAZI

There is no *personal* truth in Germany, Frau Kollwitz. There is only the truth of the whole people, which our leaders speak for us! But we wish to learn the name of the other artist most of all. It is important to keep a list of those who might be disloyal, might cause trouble in the future, to keep them under *surveillance*, perhaps even remove them for a time, in order to "rehabilitate" them.

KATHE KOLLWITZ

I will never give it to you. I know what you
have in mind.

NAZI

Do you think that we *will*, that we *can*, let
you defy us? No! Do not hope that your
age, or anything else, will save you.

KATHE KOLLWITZ

I cannot do it!

*(Kathe Kollwitz sits down in a chair and
stares off into space)*

NAZI

(He walks over to her, circling her chair.)
What is this around your neck, Frau
Kollwitz?

*(He pulls on a small cord and a pouch
appears over her neckline)*

What is this?

(She is silent and turns away. He sneers.)
Perhaps you don't think I *know*? I am no
fool -- you carry *poison* around with you! It
bolsters your courage! But it is you who
are the fool. When we come for you, we
won't give you advance notice so you can

104

take this. Oh no! We may pay you a visit, in the middle of the night; or while you are at the butchers for some meat, or in the street for a stroll; and poison is always the first thing that we look for. No, we will decide when you die, and how.

KATHE KOLLWITZ

Then you take on a very serious responsibility for the State. I will *not* tell you who the other artist was, but I will give you a retraction if that will satisfy you.

NAZI

That is the least we will accept. But I should warn you that if you, or this friend of yours, is so foolish as to speak *again* to a Russian correspondent; or one from *any* other country, we will be back to see you *agai,n* and we have ways of getting people to divulge the names of people they have sworn never to reveal: husbands, fathers, even sons.

KATHE KOLLWITZ

I have no doubt of your cruelty.

NAZI

Please, Frau Kollwitz, please -- our "persuasiveness".

KATHE KOLLWITZ

Do you wish me to write it now?

NAZI

I will send somebody back tomorrow for it. *(He picks up some of her etchings lying about. Plate: 12.)*

Are these your latest work?

KATHE KOLLWITZ

Yes.

NAZI

They all seem to have to do with death.

KATHE KOLLWITZ

What else is there now for me?

NAZI

What else is there in *Germany,* now, for you, I think you mean. Hauptman came along, Frau Kollwitz, he has adapted; and we have not been unmindful of it -- he has not gone unrewarded for it -- think of that!

KATHE KOLLWITZ

I prefer to think of death.

106

NAZI

These prints are in black, it is the color of the uniforms of the elite guards. You see I was rewarded for my efforts for the party, and was even given a commission in the SS.

KATHE KOLLWITZ

You have gotten the reward you wanted -- I've no doubt of it.

NAZI

(Going over to a sideboard with some photographs on it.)

That must be your family, Frau Kollwitz. Your husband there, your son, his wife and their four children, here. I know a great deal about you, Frau Kollwitz, it is part of my job to know about the people I interrogate. You have a grandson, I believe, who is now about fourteen, or fifteen, I should think. He will be ready for the Army soon. That is the woman's job --to produce sons for the Army, to fight for Germany, when the time comes. That must be his picture there.

(He picks it up but it accidentally falls through his hands and breaks.)

I'm sorry -- what was his name?

KATHE KOLLWITZ

Peter.

NAZI

I must be going, but remember what I've said, if you wish to see *Peter* reach military age.

(He leaves.)

KATHE KOLLWITZ

I am sick.

Scene iii

(1938. The Scene takes place in the living room of the Kollwitz apartment. Hans, their son, and Ottilie, his wife, enter the room in front of the senior Kollwitz's. When they are all seated, Lina serves coffee.)

OTTILIE

Hans always looks forward to these visits, as do I.

HANS KOLLWITZ

But Mother you seem preoccupied today.

DR. KOLLWITZ

Your mother's work has been removed... again!

HANS KOLLWITZ

From the Kloster Street show? Just a show of local artists? The sculpture of the Tower of Mothers?

KATHE KOLLWITZ

Yes.

HANS KOLLWITZ

Nothing escapes them; *nothing* is too paltry!

DR. KOLLWITZ

Some had held out hope...

HANS KOLLWITZ

(Waits until Lina leaves the room.)
But why?

DR. KOLLWITZ

They didn't like the idea of the Mothers protecting their children from the military I suppose.

HANS KOLLWITZ

Is that it?

KATHE KOLLWITZ

Yes.

HANS KOLLWITZ

I mean is that what you are gloomy about?

KATHE KOLLWITZ

That is bad; but to be expected. What is depressing is the curious silence surrounding the expulsion of my work ...Scarcely anyone had anything to say to me about it.

HANS KOLLWITZ

They are afraid!

KATHE KOLLWITZ

At times I feel as if I have come to the end of my work, if no one cares what purpose to go on. One must struggle to prevent this silence from penetrating into one's soul.

110

HANS KOLLWITZ

What *could* they say?

KATHE KOLLWITZ

Something! Anything! Now people avoid each other.

DR. KOLLWITZ

People are civil when they see you, they speak of this or that, but never of anything important. They are always anxious now to leave, to be alone, and take care to keep their opinions to themselves.

HANS KOLLWITZ

I have noticed that too.

OTTILIE

It is bad for all of us, but at least we have each other.

HANS KOLLWITZ

That's true, Mother.

KATHE KOLLWITZ

Yes, I have Karl and all of you. We must clasp hands and hold tight so that we lose *no one* from our little circle.

DR. KOLLWITZ

The children have been out a long time playing.

HANS KOLLWITZ

If they do not come home soon I will go out to look for them.

(There is a knock at the door.)

OTTILIE

They are back.

KATHE KOLLWITZ

They have come to see if we have missed them yet.

DR. KOLLWITZ

And we have!

(Hans rises and goes over to open the door. Peter enters out of breath.)

PETER KOLLWITZ

Grandmother!   Grandfather!   Mother! Father!

HANS KOLLWITZ

What Peter? Where are your brother and sisters?

PETER KOLLWITZ

Outside! Father . . .

112

HANS KOLLWITZ

What *is it*, Peter?

PETER KOLLWITZ

Men, men in uniform . . .

DR. KOLLWITZ

(Alarmed)

The *Gestapo*?

PETER KOLLWITZ

No . . . The Army marching . . . a parade . . .
down the street . . . coming this way...

KATHE KOLLWITZ

Militarism. Nazis. Hitler. Worms in the
German soul!

*(Peter goes to the window and opens it. The
women go, protectively, to the window; the
men remain motionless. When the window is
opened the tramp of marching boots is heard
from the street below, loudly, menacingly.)*

Scene iv

*(1939, ballet, a street scene in Berlin. Plate
13. A group of German youth follow a soldier*

with a drum playing a military cadence. There is no other musical accompaniment and the rhythm of the drum follows that of the percussion passage introducing the second movement of Bartok's "Concerto for Orchestra". In front is a Nazi dressed in black. He points to the young worker-types who are standing around, hanging back, some trying to escape being seen; and as he beckons them, they fall in line behind the marching group in a wildly ecstatic and exaggerated march. In mime one questions, protests, then comes forward, at first reluctantly but finally joining the frenzied marching of the rest. They go off and the three old women, some other men and women, and the Kollwitzes appear. After the words of each old woman, but not the others in the scene, the drum is heard off stage.)

FIRST OLD WOMAN

Germany is rearming.

SECOND OLD WOMAN

In violation of the treaty.

THIRD OLD WOMAN

The Rhineland has been remilitarized.

FIRST CITIZEN

It is German -- why not?

SECOND CITIZEN

Hitler seizes Austria.

PETER KOLLWITZ

Czechoslovakia has been partitioned.

THIRD OLD WOMAN

Now swallowed whole.

SECOND OLD WOMAN

Germany demands a Polish corridor to Danzig.

SECOND CITIZEN

Do you want to hear the latest joke?

FIRST CITIZEN

What is it?

SECOND CITIZEN

Poland has invaded Germany.

(They both laugh uproariously and go off.)

DR. KOLLWITZ

It's war!

KATHE KOLLWITZ

It begins again.

(The stage empties except for the old women.)

PETER KOLLWITZ

Poland falls.

SECOND OLD WOMAN

Then Denmark, the low countries, and Norway.

THIRD OLD WOMAN

France is defeated. The British evacuate Europe.

SECOND OLD WOMAN

Yugoslavia and Greece fall.

PETER KOLLWITZ

Germany invades Russia!

Scene v

(1941. The three old women enter Dr. Kollwitz's waiting room. There is a sign indicating the office is "Closed". They shrug, turn around and leave.)

116

FIRST OLD WOMAN

Closed?

SECOND OLD WOMAN

Closed!

THIRD OLD WOMAN

Closed, yes, ...closed.

Scene vi

(1942. Kathe Kollwitz and her maid are in her apartment, which has now also become her studio. Kathe Kollwitz is resting in a chair, the maid, Lina, is dusting.)

LINA

Always so much dust.

KATHE KOLLWITZ

The ghost of blown up buildings.

LINA

And maybe even flesh.

KATHE KOLLWITZ

Don't say such things!

LINA

The living and the dead -- what difference now?

KATHE KOLLWITZ

Things are bad, but we must stay alive if we can.

LINA

I don't want to die but who can predict it? When the air raid sirens go off I go to shelters, like everybody else, who knows what we will see when we come out again or when some bomb that has not exploded yet, will go off.

KATHE KOLLWITZ

So far we are still alive, you and I.

(She gets up using a cane and goes to the window.)

Ah, it is a fine October day, clear and bright; just the kind that Karl liked, for a walk. He loved his walk -- no one loved it more.

(She shifts the cane from one hand to the other.)

It's hard to think it's been over two years now, another year and it would have been our 60th anniversary! I tried to hold him but he slipped away. It was his time, I suppose. We had been through so much together. I needed him but, for himself, he was ready. He had lived his life, and, since the Nazis, there wasn't much for him. I look back, and am grateful for the years we had together. The funeral was sad, but not bitter. It was sad for us who lost him, but he had lived his life as a man. People came - - all kinds of people`-- friends and patients - - many were both, to say goodbye. They all missed him -- some had stories of favors he had done for them, some even tried to put money in my hand; but I refused it, of course! Mostly they were old, and mostly poor, but some were young too, and some were well off; they had left this part of the city many years ago, but remembered, grateful for some past kindness, and returned to pay their respects. It was a sad time, but a good time; a time when people could reflect upon the goodness in the world; that such a man should have been allowed to live out his life and touch others in the fullness of it. That knowledge made it easier to accept his loss; although it's never easy. Sometimes I lose myself in the past.

LINA

What is there to give anyone pleasure now?

KATHE KOLLWITZ

I cannot understand war, but this one even less.

LINA

Your grandson, Peter, now is at the Russian front.

KATHE KOLLWITZ

It worries me all the time. I was so relieved when he was sick with jaundice and urged him to take as long as possible to recover from it.

LINA

The young heal fast.

KATHE KOLLWITZ

They should take more time at it.

LINA

They are impatient to get on with their life.

KATHE KOLLWITZ

Now he is back at the front. I urged him not to volunteer. I begged his parents to keep him home. The boy would have none of it. I cited to his Father his brother's example; but back to me he offered his own. Even his name is precious to me, and at times he looks a little like my own Peter. Sometimes it frightens me when I see the resemblance.

LINA

He's a good boy, he will be careful.

KATHE KOLLWITZ

It's not only up to him!

LINA

You will feel better when you get a letter from him.

KATHE KOLLWITZ

I haven't had one from him in awhile.

LINA

News travels slowly from the Russian front.

KATHE KOLLWITZ

It has been awhile, now, since I have seen his Father, or heard from him. Hans usually does not allow so much time to pass without a call, or visit. You know I would almost believe, because we have been speaking of him, that it is Hans coming down the street now.

LINA

(Comes near the window.)

I believe it is!

KATHE KOLLWITZ

What could bring him here today? He prefers to visit on the weekends usually, and Ottilie always comes with him, and their dear children.

LINA

Today he is a solitary messenger.

KATHE KOLLWITZ

Of what?

LINA

Perhaps what he knows keeps the rest at home.

KATHE KOLLWITZ

I begin to fill up with dread.

LINA

Maybe it is good news he has to tell us that could not wait. It could be Peter has been promoted; or been reassigned to the Western front, or maybe comes home on furlough.

KATHE KOLLWITZ

The more you put a favorable construction on it, the more it worries me. Fate often holds out some promise, then rips away the veil, to show us what makes us *despair* instead!

LINA

I cannot see his face to read it.

KATHE KOLLWITZ

He looks neither to the right nor left, but only straight ahead. This is no pleasure visit that he comes on. He comes because he must, not because he wishes it.

LINA

You read too much into it!

KATHE KOLLWITZ

I know my son well enough after fifty years, I think. He has to tell me something he does not wish to, but cannot face me again if he does not.

(Footsteps sound on the stairs outside, then a knock. The maid opens it.)

HANS KOLLWITZ

(Softly.)

Lina, where is Mother?

(She points then leaves the room.)

KATHE KOLLWITZ

(After a silence and still looking out the window.)

Hello, Hans.

HANS KOLLWITZ

Good Morning, Mother.

(Brief silence.)

I have bad news to tell you.

KATHE KOLLWITZ

Peter's been killed.

HANS KOLLWITZ

(He covers the tears in his eyes, then regaining his control.)

124

How did you know?

KATHE KOLLWITZ

I knew -- I'm sorry for you.

(Plate 15)

Scene vii

*(1943. The Setting is the same as at the end
of Act I, Scene i.)*

DRIVER

Have you left *anything* behind?

KATHE KOLLWITZ

Have I left something behind?

DRIVER

Yes!

KATHE KOLLWITZ

No -- I carry it *all* with me.

(She turns and leaves and he follows.)

THE END

The biographical information about the life of Kathe Kollwitz was obtained from the following sources:

Mina C. Klein and H. Arthur Klein, *Kathe Kollwitz, Life in Art*, Holt Rinehart and Winston, 1972; Martha Kearns, *Kathe Kollwitz: Woman and Artist*, The Feminist Press, 1976; and *The Diary and Letters of Kaethe Kollwitz* edited by Hans Kollwitz, translated by Richard and Clara Winston, Henry Regnery Company, 1955; George H. Pollock, M.D., Ph.D., "The Mourning-Liberation Process and Creativity: The Case of Kathe Kollwitz", in *The Annual of Psychoanalysis Volume X*, International Universities Press, 1982.

Plates

1.   Self Portrait (1933)

2.   Self Portrait with son Hans at the table (1894

3.   A Weaver's Rebellion leaf 2 Death (1897)

4.   A Weaver's Rebellion leaf 3 Conspiracy (1898)

5.   A Weaver's Rebellion leaf 4 March of the Weavers (1897)

6.   A Weaver's Rebellion leaf 6 The End (1897)

7.   Mother with Dead Child (1903) Etching

8.   Berlin Casualty Lists WW I

9.   The parents

10.   In Memoriam Karl Liebnecht (1920) Woodcut

11.   Hunger Poster (1923)

12.. Never Again War (1924) Poster

13.   Death leaf 8 Death Calls (1934-35)

14.   War leaf 2 The Volunteers (1922-23)

15.. Seed for the Planting Must Not Be
      Ground Up (1942)

16.   Gravestone   Franz   Levy   (1938)
      Jewish cemetery, Cologne

Self Portrait 1933

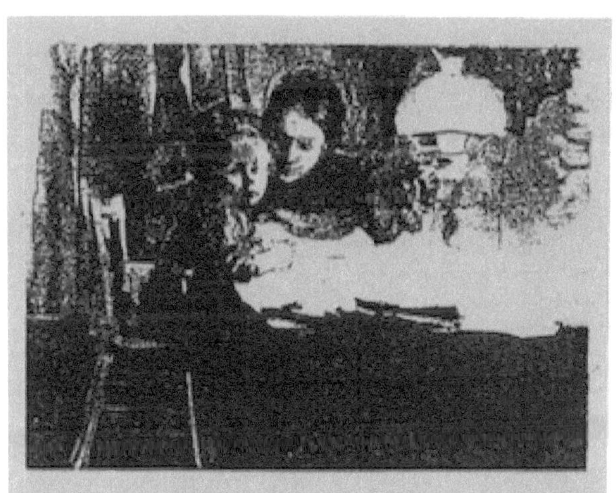

Kathe Kollwitz with Hans (1894)

Weavers – Sick Child

Weavers – Conspiracy

Weavers – March

Weavers – Defeat

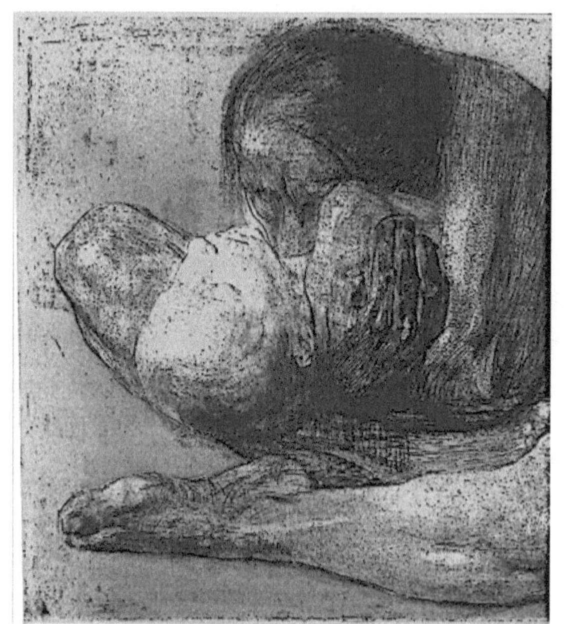

Mother with dead Child

Casualties posted, WW I Berlin

Grieving Parents

In Memoriam Karl Liebnecht

Hunger

Nie Wieder Krieg

Death Calls

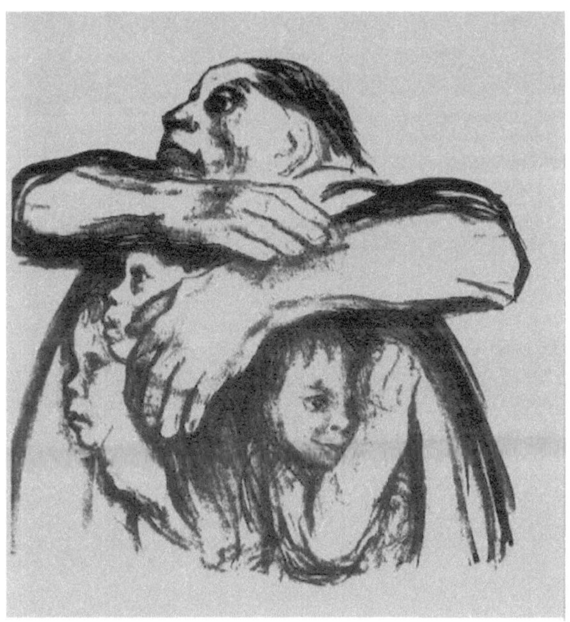

Seed for the Planting

Volunteers

Gravestone Franz Levy (1938